Visual Geography Series®

AUSTRIA

...in Pictures

Prepared by
Geography Department

Lerner Publications Company
Minneapolis

Independent Picture Service

Hydroelectric plants harness the power of rapid streams flowing in the Austrian Alps.

This book is an all-new edition in the Visual Geography Series. Previous editions were published by Sterling Publishing Company, New York City. The text, set in 10/12 Century Textbook, is fully revised and updated, and new photographs, maps, charts, and captions have been added.

LIBRARY OF CONGRESS CATALOGING-IN-PUBLICATION DATA

Austria in pictures / prepared by Geography Department, Lerner Publications Company.
    p. cm. — (Visual geography series)
    Rev. ed. of: Austria in pictures / prepared by Edgar S. Bley.
    Includes index.
    Summary: Text and photographs introduce the topography, history, society, economy, and governmental structure of Austria.
    ISBN 0-8225-1888-0 (lib. bdg.)
    1. Austria. 2. Austria—Pictorial works. [1. Austria.] I. Bley, Edgar S. Austria in pictures II. Lerner Publications Company. Geography Dept. III. Series: Visual geography series (Minneapolis, Minn.).
DB17.A83 1991
914.36'0022'2—dc20   91-7448
                               CIP
                               AC

International Standard Book Number: 0-8225-1888-0
Library of Congress Catalog Card Number: 91-7448

VISUAL GEOGRAPHY SERIES®

Publisher
Harry Jonas Lerner
Associate Publisher
Nancy M. Campbell
Senior Editor
Mary M. Rodgers
Editors
Gretchen Bratvold
Dan Filbin
Tom Streissguth
Photo Researcher
Kerstin Coyle
Editorial/Photo Assistants
Marybeth Campbell
Colleen Sexton
Consultants/Contributors
William J. McGrath
Sandra K. Davis
Designer
Jim Simondet
Cartographer
Carol F. Barrett
Indexers
Kristine S. Schubert
Sylvia Timian
Production Manager
Gary J. Hansen

Independent Picture Service

Many residents of Neusiedl am See, in eastern Austria, use reeds from the shores of the nearby Neusiedler See to roof their homes.

Acknowledgments

Title page photo © David Falconer.

Elevation contours adapted from *The Times Atlas of the World,* seventh comprehensive edition (New York: Times Books, 1985).

1 2 3 4 5 6 7 8 9 10 00 99 98 97 96 95 94 93 92 91

A ferry on the busy Danube River runs between Passau, on Austria's border with Germany, and the Austrian city of Linz. The Danube has been an important transportation route in central Europe since prehistoric times.

Contents

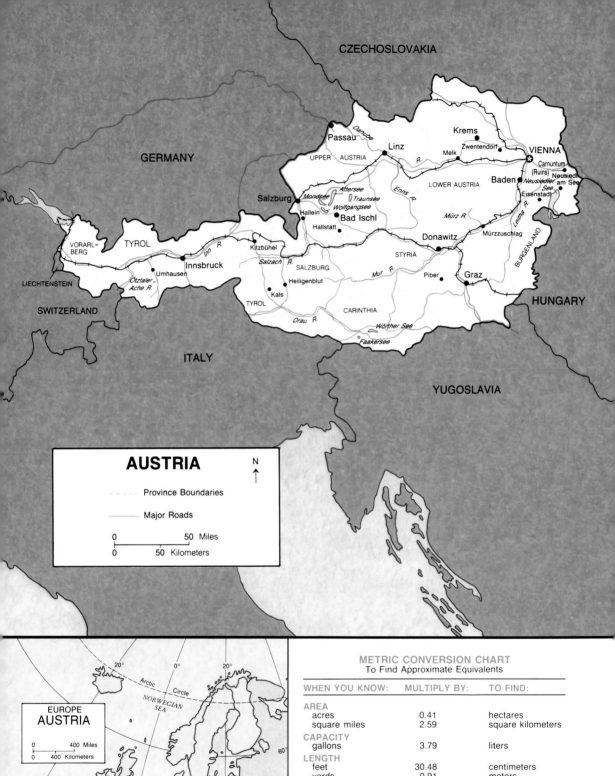

CZECHOSLOVAKIA

GERMANY

Passau
Danube
Linz
Krems
Zwentendorf
Melk
R.
VIENNA
Carnuntum
(Ruins)
Neusiedl am See
UPPER AUSTRIA
LOWER AUSTRIA
Baden
Neusiedler See
Eisenstadt

Salzburg
Mondsee
Attersee
Traunsee
Wolfgangsee
Hallein
Bad Ischl
Hallstatt
Enns R.
Mürz R.
Donawitz
Mürzzuschlag
Leitha R.

VORARL-BERG
TYROL
Inn R.
Kitzbühel
Salzach R.
SALZBURG
STYRIA
Piber
Graz
BURGENLAND

LIECHTENSTEIN
Innsbruck
Umhausen
Ötztaler Ache R.
Heiligenblut
Mur R.

SWITZERLAND
Kals
TYROL
CARINTHIA
Drau R.
Wörther See
Faakersee
HUNGARY

ITALY

YUGOSLAVIA

AUSTRIA

N

- - - - Province Boundaries

———— Major Roads

0   50   Miles

0   50   Kilometers

EUROPE
AUSTRIA

0   400   Miles
0   400   Kilometers

Arctic Circle
NORWEGIAN SEA
NORTH ATLANTIC OCEAN
MEDITERRANEAN SEA

20° 0° 20° 60° 20° 40° 0° 20°

METRIC CONVERSION CHART
To Find Approximate Equivalents

WHEN YOU KNOW:	MULTIPLY BY:	TO FIND:
AREA		
acres	0.41	hectares
square miles	2.59	square kilometers
CAPACITY		
gallons	3.79	liters
LENGTH		
feet	30.48	centimeters
yards	0.91	meters
miles	1.61	kilometers
MASS (weight)		
pounds	0.45	kilograms
tons	0.91	metric tons
VOLUME		
cubic yards	0.77	cubic meters
TEMPERATURE		
degrees Fahrenheit	0.56 (*after* subtracting 32)	degrees Celsius

Many farmers in the valleys of the Austrian Alps must cope with uneven, rocky fields and a short growing season. Nevertheless, Alpine highlands support grain fields as well as pastures. After cutting, this hay crop is dried in stacks before storage.

Photo by Daniel H. Condit

Introduction

The Republic of Austria is a landlocked, mountainous nation of 7.7 million people in central Europe. Once part of a huge empire that ruled many different ethnic groups, Austria now consists of nine small provinces in which the dominant language is German.

The history of Austria has been shaped by the country's location at a crossroads of European trade and migration. The Danube River, which runs through northern Austria, links western, northern, and eastern Europe. The earliest settlers in the Danube Valley were Celts from the east

and Romans from the Italian Peninsula to the south. In the 1200s, Rudolf of Habsburg founded a dynasty (family of rulers) that controlled Austria and other European lands for more than 600 years.

At its height in the sixteenth and seventeenth centuries, the Habsburg Empire included nearly half of Europe. Eventually, however, the empire's non-German ethnic groups won their independence from Habsburg rule.

In 1914, as a result of unrest in central Europe, several European nations were drawn into World War I. Austria joined its

5

neighbor Germany and battled Italy, Serbia, and Russia. After four years of fighting, Austria and Germany lost the war, and the Habsburg dynasty collapsed. In 1918 the victors of World War I divided the empire into several new, independent countries—one of which was the Republic of Austria.

Weakened by a severe economic depression in the late 1920s and early 1930s, Austria was unable to stop a takeover by Germany in 1938. When World War II broke out in 1939, Austria fought with Germany against the allied powers of Britain, the United States, and the Soviet Union. After extensive bombing and ground attacks by the Allies, Austria and Germany surrendered in 1945.

With foreign aid, Austria slowly rebuilt its economy. By 1955 the country had achieved steady economic growth and a stable government. To safeguard this recovery, Austria's leaders declared that the nation would not take sides in any future European conflicts.

Modern Austrians enjoy a high standard of living. Health insurance and social-security benefits cover all workers, and the rate of unemployment is low. Members of the country's leading political parties cooperate in setting national policies, and Austria's trade with both eastern and western Europe is increasing. As a prosperous democracy located in the center of a large European market, Austria has a promising economic future.

Independent Picture Service

An artisan puts the finishing touches on detailed statuettes produced at the Augarten porcelain factory in Vienna, the Austrian capital city.

The Faakersee, in the southern province of Carinthia, is one of a series of lakes lying in the valley of the Drau River. Wooded highlands surround the narrow valley, which has the warmest climate in Austria.

1) The Land

Austria lies between the Alps, Europe's highest mountain range, and the plains of northern and eastern Europe. Rivers and mountains form most of the country's borders. Switzerland and Liechtenstein border Austria to the west, and Germany sits to the north. Austria's eastern European neighbors are Czechoslovakia in the northeast, Hungary in the east, and Yugoslavia in the southeast. To the south, across a high mountain barrier, lies Italy.

Austria's total land area of 32,374 square miles makes it slightly smaller than the state of Maine. The country's greatest distance from north to south is about 180 miles. From west to east, Austria measures 355 miles.

Topography

Mountains and uplands occupy about 70 percent of Austria. The Alps dominate the country's western, southern, and central regions. Although less mountainous, Austria's eastern and northern provinces contain rugged hills and dense forests. Most Austrians live in lowland regions and river valleys.

Photo © Thomas Henion

Heiligenblut, a village in Carinthia, lies in the shadow of Grossglockner, the highest peak in the Austrian Alps.

THE ALPS

The Austrian Alps extend from the Swiss border nearly to the Danube River. Broad valleys divide these highlands into northern, central, and southern ranges.

The northern Austrian Alps run from the western province of Vorarlberg to the suburbs of Vienna, Austria's capital. The central Alps include smaller mountain groups such as the Ötztaler, the Zillertaler, the Hohe Tauern, and the Niedere Tauern ranges. Grossglockner, the country's high-est peak, rises 12,460 feet above sea level in the Hohe Tauern Alps. Glaciers (slow-moving ice masses) and permanent snow-fields exist on many of these mountains, where temperatures often stay below freezing even in summer.

The southern Alps parallel Austria's boundaries with Italy and Yugoslavia. These highlands, which include the border range of the Karawanken Mountains, sur-round the valley of the Drau River in the southern province of Carinthia.

Narrow passes cross the Alps in several places. The passes ease transportation within Austria and provide a vital link to neighboring countries. The Brenner Pass in the western province of Tyrol has long been an important route for travelers go-ing from Germany and Austria to Italy. The Arlberg Pass connects Switzerland and Vorarlberg to Tyrol and the rest of Austria. In the east, the Semmering Pass carries traffic between Vienna and south-ern Austria.

EASTERN AND NORTHERN AUSTRIA

A series of foothills marks the southeast-ern limit of the Austrian Alps. Burgenland, a long and narrow eastern province that borders Hungary, consists of low hills and level plains. The Neusiedler See (lake) in Burgenland lies at 377 feet above sea level —the country's lowest elevation. North of Burgenland is the Vienna Basin, a farm-ing region that surrounds the capital. The Weinviertel (wine district) north of Vien-na is an important wine-producing area.

Northwest of Vienna, a plateau extends from the Danube River to the Czech bor-der. The Waldviertel (wooded district) and the Mühlviertel (mill district) are hilly, for-ested regions north of the Danube. Foot-hills run from the northern Alps to the Danube Valley, creating high banks and narrow passages in several places along the river. The Salzkammergut—a region of steep slopes and narrow glacial lakes—lies just north of the Alps near Austria's fron-tier with Germany.

Rivers and Lakes

Austria's rivers serve as important transportation routes within this landlocked country. The major rivers, which are tributaries of the Danube, run west to east between high mountain ridges.

The Danube begins in Germany and crosses the Austrian border near the city of Passau. The river flows 217 miles through the provinces of Upper Austria and Lower Austria before entering Czechoslovakia. Vineyards and hillside fields line the Danube west of Vienna, where a canal diverts the river's waters toward the city. Once famous for its deep blue color, the Danube is now muddy and brown from pollutants that have contaminated it during the past two centuries.

Each spring, melting snow swells the 317-mile Inn River, which begins in the

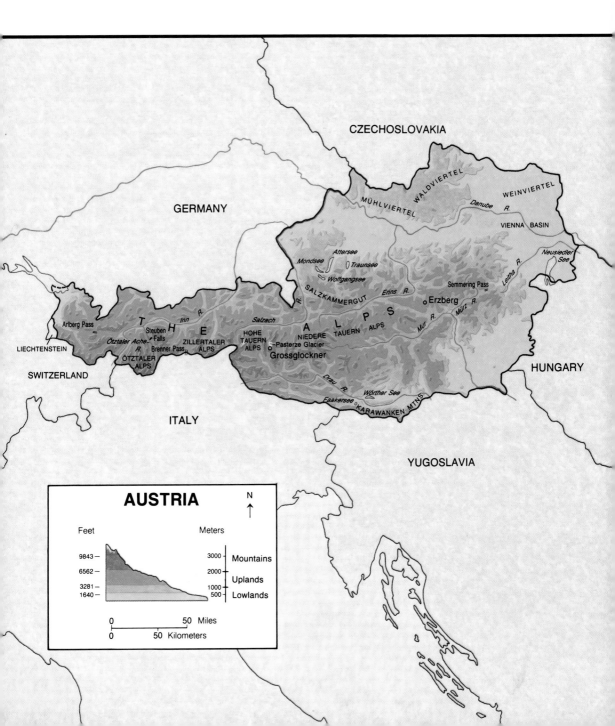

mountains of eastern Switzerland. After winding northeastward through Tyrol, the Inn crosses into Germany and then turns eastward to form the German-Austrian boundary. The Salzach River passes through the city of Salzburg and marks a portion of the German border before emptying into the Inn.

Farther east, the Enns River flows through central Austria for 158 miles before joining the Danube east of the city of Linz. The Mur River rises in the central Alps and runs eastward through the Niedere Tauern range. After turning south, the Mur passes the city of Graz and enters Yugoslavia. The Mur and the Mürz are the principal rivers of Styria, an important industrial and mining province of southeastern Austria.

In northern and southern Austria, groups of long, narrow lakes lie in broad valleys between the mountains. The lakes of the Salzkammergut region in Upper Austria have become a popular resort area. The largest of these lakes are the Mondsee, the Attersee, and the Traunsee. Lakes surrounded by steep mountains also dot the Drau River Valley in Carinthia. Two of these lakes—the Faakersee and the Wörther See—draw many visitors to this southern province.

The shallow Neusiedler See is more than 20 miles long and about 5 miles wide. The lake, which lies on Austria's border with Hungary, attracts a variety of freshwater birds. Thick reeds from the lake's shoreline provide thatch, a material used to make the roofs of houses in nearby towns.

Fed by melting snow, the mountain streams of Austria flood the high valleys during the early spring. At Steuben Falls near Umhausen, the Ötztaler Ache River rushes down a steep gorge toward its junction with the Inn River in Tyrol.

Spoonbills nest along the shores of the Neusiedler See. Many of Europe's freshwater birds inhabit this shallow, reedy lake on Austria's border with Hungary.

Flora and Fauna

Forests cover nearly 40 percent of Austria. Beech, oak, and birch grow in the lower altitudes, and Carinthia's milder climate supports wild fruit and nut trees. Spruce, fir, larch, and pine thrive on the mountain slopes up to the timberline. Above the timberline, low temperatures and short summers prevent the growth of trees. Wildflowers such as edelweiss, gentian, primrose, buttercup, and monkshood flourish at high elevations.

Hunters have eliminated nearly all of Austria's bears, wolves, and wild boars, which were once abundant in the country's forests. A small European deer called the roebuck survives, as does the marmot (a small, burrowing rodent), the hare, and the chamois (an agile, antelope-like animal). To preserve these species, the Austrian government enforces strict hunting laws.

A wide variety of birds live in the country's mountainous regions. Ptarmigans,

The European roebuck is Austria's largest wild animal. Protected from hunting, the roebucks graze in the highlands of Upper Austria and in other mountainous areas of the country.

11

snow finches, and eagles nest in Tyrol and in the highlands near Salzburg. The Neusiedler See in eastern Austria is home to egrets, herons, storks, and spoonbills.

Various species of fish—including trout, char, pike, catfish, and perch—inhabit Austria's lakes. Strict environmental laws have kept these waters fairly clean. Trout and grayling are two sport fish found in Alpine streams.

Climate

Austria's climate varies with both terrain and season. Winds that blow eastward from Europe's Atlantic coast moderate temperatures in the country's mountainous western and central provinces. The higher elevations and mountain passes are generally colder than the river valleys.

Summers in the Alps are short but warm, with frequent, sudden storms. Winters

Courtesy of Austrian National Tourist Office

Snow often blankets Schloss Belvedere, an eighteenth-century palace in Vienna. Winter precipitation reaches cities in the river valleys as well as the mountainous regions of Austria.

Passenger ferries, sailboats, and speedboats ply Austria's inland waters. On this lake in the Salzkammergut, a boathouse shelters vessels from the storms and high waves that can arise suddenly in any season.

tend to be long, but clear and dry days are common. Rainfall in Innsbruck, a city in the central Alps, averages 34 inches per year. In winter, most of Innsbruck's precipitation falls as snow. The city's temperatures average 27° F in January, the coldest month, and 66° F in July, the warmest month.

Winds blowing from eastern Europe bring a drier climate to Vienna and the eastern provinces. In the capital, temperatures average 29° F in January and 68° F in July. Spring and fall are mild and cloudy. Vienna gets about 26 inches of rainfall each year. The provinces of Styria and Carinthia are the country's sunniest and driest regions.

In fall and spring, warm air currents called the föhn winds blow across the Alps from the south. These winds sometimes bring fog and a quick rise in temperature to mountain valleys throughout the country. Warm enough to melt snow at high elevations, the föhn winds can cause dangerous avalanches—huge masses of falling snow—on the Alpine mountainsides.

Glaciers are slow-moving masses of snow and ice that flow along the highest mountain valleys. Austria's Pasterze Glacier lies near the slopes of Grossglockner in Carinthia.

13

Natural Resources

Austria possesses a variety of natural resources. The country's most valuable minerals are coal and iron ore, both of which are mined in Styria. Lower Austria has reserves of crude oil and natural gas. A large refinery near Vienna supplies about 10 percent of the country's petroleum.

Austria is a leading producer of magnesite, a mineral used in the manufacture of building materials. Austrian factories also use high-grade graphite to make pencils and industrial equipment. The country's other mineral resources include copper, lead, zinc, bauxite (which is used to make aluminum), salt, and quartz.

Tree conservation and replanting efforts have allowed Austria to preserve much of its forested land. Loggers harvest spruce and fir, the most commercially valuable trees, for export and for domestic use. Swift rivers power hydroelectric stations on the Enns, Drau, Mur, and Danube rivers. Austria sells surplus electricity from these plants to neighboring countries.

Workers emerge from the salt mines at Hallein in the province of Salzburg. Salt deposits in the region have been worked for at least 2,000 years. Once extremely valuable, salt is now a minor resource for the Austrian economy.

Dams along the Danube River supply electricity to nearby cities and to many industries. The barriers have slowed the course of the river, where navigation was once made difficult by rapids.

The Kärntner Strasse, one of the main streets of central Vienna, has been converted into a pedestrian zone where motorized vehicles are prohibited. Many shops occupy the lower floors of the buildings that line this route.

Vienna

Vienna, the capital of Austria, sits on the southern bank of the Danube River about

Surrounded by a spacious park, Vienna's nineteenth-century Rathaus, or city hall, houses the offices of the city's mayor and of many civic departments.

40 miles from the country's border with Czechoslovakia. The capital has a population of 1.5 million—roughly one-fifth of the nation's people. The many palaces and historic buildings in and near the city reflect Vienna's past importance as the seat of power of the Habsburg rulers.

Vienna lies along an important trade route in central Europe. The Celts established the first settlement on the site more than 2,000 years ago. In 15 B.C., soldiers from the Roman Empire built a stronghold called Vindobona over the Celtic town. The center of Austrian government since the thirteenth century, Vienna also became the nation's cultural and industrial capital.

The "Ring," a series of wide and busy roads, surrounds the oldest parts of the city. A mile outside the Ring is a second circle of avenues, called the Gürtel (meaning "belt"). Many of Vienna's newer apartments and office buildings were built along the Gürtel.

15

Otto Wagner, a twentieth-century Austrian architect, designed this railroad pavilion in Vienna. Behind the building rises the Karlskirche, a baroque church created by Johann Fischer von Erlach.

The Viennese have rebuilt many landmarks that were damaged in bombing raids during World War II. St. Stephen's Cathedral, which dates to the fifteenth century, still towers over the city's center. The National Opera House is one of many imposing structures raised in the 1800s along the Ring. The Hofburg and Schönbrunn palaces, where Austrian monarchs once lived, now house various historical and art collections.

The chief industrial city of Austria, Vienna produces machinery, chemicals, textiles, electrical equipment, food products, and various handicrafts. Vienna is also home to a large university and to art and music academies. The city has become an important site for international negotiations and peace conferences. Several agencies of the United Nations have offices in Vienna.

Secondary Cities

Graz (population 250,000), the capital of Styria, is the site of a large fortress that

Michaelertor in Vienna is part of the massive Hofburg. The Habsburg rulers, who governed the country for more than 600 years, started building the palace in the 1200s.

One of Salzburg's oldest streets, the Getreidegasse is still a thriving commercial center. The Austrian composer Wolfgang Amadeus Mozart was born at Number 9 Getreidegasse in 1756.

Independent Picture Service

once defended Vienna and the Habsburg Empire from invading Turkish armies. Graz is now an industrial center with chemical plants, ironworks, steelworks, and automobile factories that employ many local people. Miners also extract iron ore and coal from deposits near the city.

Situated on the Danube, Linz (population 200,000) has been a river port and trading center since Roman times. The city was once an important trading post that linked northern and western Europe with countries to the east and south. The first railroad in Austria connected Linz with Czechoslovakia in 1832. Large industrial complexes in Linz produce heavy machinery, chemicals, and steel.

Courtesy of LeeAnne Engfer

Central Salzburg lies along both sides of the Salzach River. Until 1802 Salzburg was an independent principality under the control of prince-archbishops, who answered only to the head of the Roman Catholic Church.

Salzburg (population 138,000), named for a nearby salt-mining region, lies on the Salzach River near the German border. Salzburg celebrates its most famous citizen, the eighteenth-century composer Wolfgang Amadeus Mozart, in an annual summer festival that draws music lovers from all over the world. A large fortress dominates the inner city, which also has several historic churches and squares.

Innsbruck (population 116,000) is the chief city of Tyrol. Founded in the thirteenth century, Innsbruck grew as a trading post along an important road between northern Europe and Italy. The Winter Olympic Games of 1964 and 1976 were held in and around this Alpine city. The facilities built by the Austrians for the games still attract winter sports enthusiasts to the region.

Pedestrians rest beneath a statue of the Habsburg Archduke Johann on the Hauptplatz, the central square of Graz in southeastern Austria. Overlooking the square is the city's famous clocktower, which was built in 1588.

This Roman tower lies on the banks of the Danube River opposite the city of Melk. The Romans constructed forts along the Danube in the first century B.C., after establishing the river as the northern frontier of their vast European empire.

2) History and Government

In about 10,000 B.C., the glaciers that had carved many of Austria's mountain valleys began to melt and retreat from central Europe. The gradually warming climate allowed early inhabitants, who lived in caves, to survive by hunting and farming in the region's forests and valleys.

Over the centuries, people began to mine the area's salt deposits and to make metal tools and weapons. By 3000 B.C., these activities had made Austria a hub of European trade. About 800 B.C., an important commercial center developed near Hallstatt, in the Salzkammergut region. The skilled craftspeople who worked near Hallstatt exported iron and bronze swords to western and northern Europe.

After 450 B.C., invaders known as Celts moved across Europe from the east into the territory of Austria. Skilled horse riders and warriors, the Celts established the kingdom of Noricum south of the Danube River. Celtic artisans used iron, copper, and bronze to make their weapons and household utensils. Control of salt and iron-ore mines made Noricum a strong and stable kingdom for several centuries.

Roman Austria

The Celtic lands lay between the growing Roman Empire (in modern Italy) and Germanic states in northern Europe. The Celts could not stop frequent Germanic raids on Noricum's mines and settlements. After passing through the kingdom, the Germanic invaders often moved on to Roman cities that lay to the south.

To prevent these attacks, the Romans invaded Noricum in the first century B.C. By 15 B.C., they had defeated the Celts and were building new strongholds along the Danube. The Romans established three provinces in the region—Raetia in the western Alps, Noricum in central Austria, and Pannonia, which lay east of Noricum and south of the Danube.

The Romans set up a stable military administration over the Celts. For 200 years, the Roman provinces in Austria remained peaceful, and new towns were founded along the area's busy trade routes. Merchants exported salt, metals, wool, and livestock to other parts of the empire. The Romans built walled cities at Vindobona (modern Vienna) and at Carnuntum, farther east.

In the late second century A.D., however, Noricum's prosperous towns again became targets for warlike peoples living beyond the Roman frontiers. Raids across the Danube continued through the fourth century, while divisions within the Roman leadership weakened Rome's hold on its territories. As the Roman Empire lost control of the frontier provinces, trade in the region gradually declined.

At the same time, Christian missionaries were bringing their new religion to the distant cities and outposts of the empire. Although Roman emperors made harsh laws to persecute Christians, the missionaries gained many converts. By the end of the fourth century, Christianity had be-

The Romans raised arches, like this one at Carnuntum near Vienna, to commemorate their victories and to glorify their emperors.

come the official religion of the Roman Empire.

In the 400s, Roman armies withdrew from the northern provinces. Slavs from the east and Germans from the north then attacked and defeated the inhabitants of the Roman towns. After the decline of Rome in the late fifth century, a huge army of Asian Huns, led by Attila, swept through central Europe. Competition for farmland and trade routes also caused frequent wars. German-speaking peoples conquered Noricum and Raetia, and Slavs settled in Pannonia. Bohemians from the northeast pushed into the Danube River Valley, and the Alemanni, who came from the Rhine River Valley, established villages in the Alps of western Austria.

Christianity and Charlemagne

Despite the frequent warfare and invasions in the region, Christian missionaries continued to arrive in the sixth and seventh centuries. By the eighth century, the Christian faith had been organized under a single authority, the Roman Catholic Church. The church was led by a pope, who lived and worked in Rome. Many Catholic missionaries from Bavaria—a German territory north of the Alps—began moving into what is now Austria. These settlers built a new cathedral in Salzburg, a town lying between Austria and Bavaria. In 798 the pope made Salzburg the independent see (headquarters) of a Catholic archbishop.

In the late eighth century, Charlemagne, the Christian emperor of the Germanic Franks, was extending his domain eastward. After taking control of Austria in 788, Charlemagne proclaimed it an Ost Mark, meaning "east march." This was a protective zone meant to stop attacks on the Frankish Empire by eastern peoples, such as the Slavs and the Avars. Eventually the name Ost Mark changed to Österreich (meaning "eastern empire"), the modern German name for Austria.

Photo by Bettmann Archive

Attila and his army of Asian Huns devastated cities throughout Europe in the fifth century A.D. Many of Attila's raids took place in the Danube River Valley.

Photo by Bettmann Archive

Having conquered most of western Europe, including Austria, in the late 700s, Charlemagne (center) founded many schools to educate his new subjects. In this engraving, Charlemagne visits one of the new schools to test the students.

This crown was used in the coronation ceremonies of the Holy Roman emperors from the tenth century until the empire's fall in the early nineteenth century.

After Charlemagne's death in 814, his heirs fought among themselves for control of the empire. In 817 Austria became part of Bavaria, a kingdom ruled by Louis the German, a grandson of Charlemagne. But disputes and civil wars continued among Charlemagne's many descendants. The Treaty of Verdun, which was drawn up in 843 to settle the fighting, placed Bavaria in the East Frankish Kingdom. This realm stretched from Austria to the seacoast of northwestern Europe and included much of modern Germany.

After Louis's death in 876, conflicts among his heirs weakened the kingdom's defenses. At the end of the ninth century, invaders destroyed many Austrian cities and farming estates. The Magyars, a nomadic people from Asia, advanced along the Danube Valley, while Slavs and Avars attacked from the east and southeast. After the German king Otto I defeated the Magyars at the Battle of the Lech in 955, he made Austria an independent state.

The Babenberg Dynasty

In 962 the Roman Catholic pope crowned Otto as the first ruler of the Holy Roman Empire. This new empire was made up of many smaller kingdoms and principalities (realms of princes) in Italy and central Europe. Seven electors, who ruled the most important German states, voted for the emperor. In 976 Otto II, who succeeded Otto I as Holy Roman emperor, appointed Leopold of Babenberg to be the margrave (ruler) of Austria. Leopold became the first member of the Babenberg dynasty.

Under the early Babenbergs, many Bavarians moved into Austria to build new villages and farms. The Babenbergs set up a defensive frontier at the Leitha River between Austria and the Magyar lands to the east. A system of new roads expanded the country's trade with neighboring states. Although Austria remained a part of the Holy Roman Empire, the Babenbergs kept their territory largely independent.

By the mid-1100s, conflict over territory and political power was increasing between the pope and the Holy Roman emperor. The Babenbergs supported the emperor in these disputes. In 1156 Emperor Friedrich I rewarded the Babenbergs by proclaiming their territory a duchy (the domain of a duke). Heinrich II Jasomirgott, the first duke of Austria, was also the first of Austria's leaders to live permanently in Vienna. By the end of his reign in 1177, Austria had achieved peace and prosperity.

The Babenbergs also supported the Crusades—religious campaigns first called by the pope in 1095. During the Crusades, Christian knights and armies fought against non-Christian Muslims for control of Jerusalem and other holy sites in the Middle East. By the end of the twelfth century, the Danube had become a principal route to the east for the crusaders, and the economic importance of the duchy of Austria increased. Several new towns, such as Linz and Krems, flourished along the busy river. Through an agreement with the

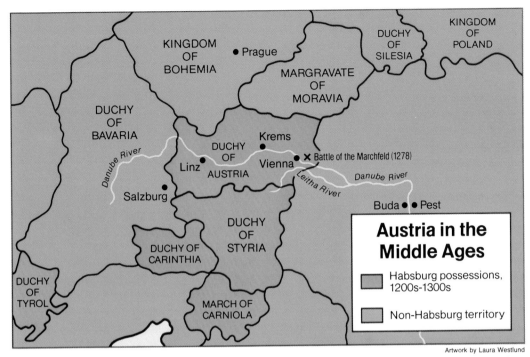

KINGDOM
OF
BOHEMIA

• Prague

DUCHY
OF
SILESIA

KINGDOM
OF
POLAND

MARGRAVATE
OF
MORAVIA

DUCHY
OF
BAVARIA

Danube River

DUCHY
OF
AUSTRIA

Krems
•

Linz
•

Vienna
•

✗ Battle of the Marchfeld (1278)

Leitha River

Danube River

Salzburg
•

Buda • • Pest

DUCHY OF
CARINTHIA

DUCHY
OF
STYRIA

**Austria in the
Middle Ages**

Habsburg possessions,
1200s-1300s

Non-Habsburg territory

DUCHY
OF
TYROL

MARCH OF
CARNIOLA

Artwork by Laura Westlund

By the thirteenth century, Austrian territory was a patchwork of small states under the control of independent rulers. Eventually, the Habsburgs—a wealthy family from Switzerland—established a dynasty in the region and combined these states under Habsburg rule.

duke of Styria, who died without an heir, the Babenbergs gained control of his duchy in 1192.

The Rise of the Habsburgs

As the duchy of Austria expanded, it faced renewed attacks by the Magyars, who killed Duke Friedrich II in battle in 1246. Friedrich, who left no heir, was the last member of the Babenberg dynasty. Ottokar II, who ruled the kingdom of Bohemia to the north, married Friedrich's widow and added Austria and Styria to his domain.

Opposing Ottokar's claim to Austria, however, was Rudolf of Habsburg, the leader of a wealthy family from Switzerland. In 1273 the German electors chose Rudolf as Holy Roman emperor. Habsburg armies then invaded Austria and defeated Ottokar at the Battle of the Marchfeld in 1278. By 1283 most of Ottokar's lands had come under Rudolf's control. The Habsburg dynasty that began with Rudolf I lasted for more than 600 years. Most of the Habsburg rulers of Austria also became Holy Roman emperors.

Through marriages, the Habsburgs added Carinthia, Tyrol, and Vorarlberg to the duchy in the fourteenth century. Yet the Habsburgs were not absolute rulers of the new provinces. Each of these territories already had its own local diet (parliament), composed of landowners and members of the Roman Catholic clergy. The clergy recognized the Roman Catholic pope as their only authority.

The diets and the landowning nobility had the power to tax the people and to raise armies. The peasants who worked for the landowners had to pay both taxes and a portion of their harvest to the nobles. The peasants could not move or marry without the permission of the nobles whose land they worked.

Although the Habsburgs were successful in adding territory to the duchy of Austria, they did not arrange for an orderly succession. Disputes among Habsburg heirs often threw the duchy into turmoil. These conflicts further weakened Habsburg authority over Austrian landowners. The rivalry between the Habsburgs and the nobles continued into the early 1400s, causing the Austrian economy to decline.

EXPANSION OF THE EMPIRE

A dispute that began in 1457 over the Habsburg succession quickly developed into a civil war. In 1463 Friedrich of Styria emerged from the conflict as the ruler of all Austrian lands except Tyrol. In 1477

Courtesy of The Cleveland Museum of Art, John L. Severance Fund

Maximilian I enlarged the Habsburg lands by shrewd marriage alliances. Through his own marriage in 1477 to Mary of Burgundy, much of northwestern Europe, including modern Belgium and the Netherlands, passed to Habsburg control.

Friedrich arranged for the marriage of his son Maximilian to Mary, heiress to the wealthy duchy of Burgundy in northern Europe. After Mary's death, Burgundian lands became Habsburg territory.

Maximilian I, who ruled from 1493 to 1519, continued to expand the Habsburg domain through marriage alliances. He arranged for his son and daughter to marry the children of the Spanish rulers Ferdinand and Isabella. Maximilian's grandson Charles V then inherited the Spanish throne in 1516. Elected Holy Roman emperor in 1519, Charles eventually brought new German, Spanish, Dutch, and Italian lands under Habsburg control.

Through marriage, Charles's brother Ferdinand I became king of Bohemia and of Hungary, a country to the east settled by the Magyars. Ferdinand, who succeeded Maximilian as ruler of Austria in 1521, struggled to protect his lands from invasion by Ottoman Turks. From their base in Istanbul (now in Turkey), the Turks conquered large areas of eastern Europe and were threatening to overthrow the Holy Roman Empire. They reached Vienna in 1529, but Ferdinand's forces turned them back from the capital.

Reformation and Revolt

By the mid-sixteenth century, the Habsburgs ruled a vast empire that included Austria, Belgium, the Netherlands, Italy, Spain, and much of Germany. At the same time, however, Austrian peasants were protesting heavy taxes and their obligations to landowners. In addition, many German princes sought independence from the rule of the Holy Roman emperor. Moreover, the scattered Habsburg territories were difficult to control, and Austria faced the constant threat of Turkish invasion.

Meanwhile, in northern Europe, a religious movement called the Protestant Reformation was challenging the authority of the Catholic church. New Protestant sects developed in Germany, and German

After his coronation in 1519 as Holy Roman emperor, Charles V ruled one of the largest realms in European history. Religious turmoil in Germany, however, and the unfavorable Peace of Augsburg that settled the conflict convinced Charles to give up his throne in 1556.

princes soon joined Protestant clergy in demanding changes in the church. Seeing an opportunity to gain their independence, the princes seized church lands and expelled Catholic officials. The Peace of Augsburg in 1555 temporarily settled the strife by allowing the princes to choose the official religion in their states. The treaty also permitted Ferdinand I to maintain Catholicism in Austria.

Charles V, who ruled both the Holy Roman Empire and Spain, opposed this settlement. Discouraged, Charles gave up his throne and retired to a Spanish monastery in 1556. The Habsburg dynasty was then split into two branches that ruled Spain and Austria independently.

Despite the Peace of Augsburg, the rivalry between Protestants and Catholics continued within Austria. Many peasants, townspeople, and members of the nobility supported new Protestant churches and universities. But in certain provinces, such as Tyrol, most of the people and the clergy favored a strong monarchy and the Roman Catholic Church. The Habsburgs, who saw the reform movement as a threat to their authority, maintained close ties with Catholic leaders.

In the late sixteenth century, Ferdinand II, a Habsburg heir, led military campaigns to expel the Protestants from southern Austria. Ferdinand became king of Bohemia in 1617. When he was proclaimed Holy Roman emperor in 1619, however, the Protestant Bohemians chose a German prince to replace him as their ruler. Ferdinand then attacked Bohemia, defeating his opponents in 1620.

Ferdinand II's campaign to restore Catholicism in Bohemia led to a long, bloody conflict known as the Thirty Years' War (1618–1648). Habsburg Catholic forces fought Protestant armies from many northern European states. The victories of Swedish Protestants late in the war forced Ferdinand's successor, Ferdinand III, to withdraw from the conflict. The Peace of Westphalia in 1648 reaffirmed the right of German princes to establish the religion of their choice in their own states.

Expansion and Reform

By the late 1600s, Turkish armies had returned to Austria, invading provinces east and south of Vienna. The Turks had the support of Louis XIV, the king of

A brilliant military planner, Eugene of Savoy led the forces defending Vienna against the Turks of the Ottoman Empire. In the seventeenth century, the Turks were sweeping north from their home in Asia Minor (modern Turkey). After the defeat of the Turks in 1683, Eugene directed successful campaigns against the French in northern Europe and in Italy.

France, who wanted to challenge the Habsburgs' power. When a large Turkish force attacked Vienna, the Habsburg emperor asked other nations for help. A combined force of Austrians, Germans, and Poles finally drove the Turks from the capital in 1683. After this victory, Austria gained Turkish land in southeastern Europe.

While the Austrian Habsburgs were increasing their territory, the Spanish Habsburg dynasty was ending. When Louis XIV attempted to place a member of his family on the Spanish throne, war broke out between Austria and France. The treaty that ended the war in 1713 added new territory in the Netherlands and in Italy to the Habsburg domain.

Wars with France and Turkey drained Austria of people and resources. As a result, the reign of Charles VI, which began in 1711, was marked by unrest and by economic weakness. Although he ruled the largest empire in Europe, Charles had little control over many Habsburg territories. Independent local parliaments often defied his wishes, and movements for self-rule in Hungary and Bohemia challenged his authority.

Charles, who had no direct male heir, also faced the problem of continuing his dynasty. In 1713 he drew up the Pragmatic Sanction, which allowed a woman to inherit the Habsburg throne. Upon Charles's death in 1740, his daughter Maria Theresa succeeded him without opposition. The Pragmatic Sanction originally had the support of other European powers. Soon after Maria Theresa's accession, however, the kingdom of Prussia in northern Germany attacked the wealthy Bohemian province of Silesia, a Habsburg possession. France, Spain, and other nations soon joined Prussia in the War of the Austrian Succession.

Austria was unable to defeat the stronger Prussian forces, which gained control of Silesia. Maria Theresa's later attempts to recover Silesia led to the Seven Years' War, which ended with another Prussian victory in 1763.

After the Seven Years' War, Maria Theresa turned her attention to Austria's weak and outdated economy. She supported new manufacturing industries and reduced the taxes imposed on the peasants. Maria Theresa also reformed the legal system and seized Roman Catholic property. In 1774 she established secular (nonreligious) schools that made education available to all Austrian citizens.

Joseph II, who succeeded Maria Theresa in 1780, continued these reforms. Joseph closed many Catholic monasteries and churches, declaring that his government would allow greater freedom of religion and of political expression. He further modernized Austria's industries and encouraged the immigration of skilled workers from neighboring countries. In 1781 Joseph freed the peasants from many of their duties to Austria's landowners.

Napoleon and Metternich

After Joseph's death in 1790, his successors Leopold II and Franz II repealed many of his reforms and began to strictly control writing and public speech. These rulers felt that Joseph's reforms had gone too far in changing the state's traditional institutions. Supporters of the new restrictions also saw a threat to the Austrian

Raised in Innsbruck in 1765, this triumphal arch acclaimed the marriage of the future Austrian emperor Leopold II. Symbols of mourning were added to the arch after the death of Leopold's father, Franz.

monarchy from a violent revolution that had overthrown the king of France. Seeking to expand French territory, the French revolutionary government declared war on Austria in 1792. France then seized Habsburg land in the Netherlands. By the early 1800s, the French general Napoleon Bonaparte had also conquered Habsburg territory in northern Italy and southern Germany.

To oppose the French, Franz II formed an alliance with Britain, Russia, and Prussia. By 1804, however, the Holy Roman Empire was a weak federation of states. In that year, Franz II declared himself Emperor Franz I of Austria. This new empire included the provinces of modern Austria as well as Hungary, Bohemia, and several other small states in southeastern Europe. Napoleon's victories in Germany caused the collapse of the Holy Roman Empire in 1806.

Although Napoleon successfully invaded Austria and occupied Vienna, the nations allied against him eventually defeated him. After their final victory in 1815, the allies met at the Congress of Vienna to determine the new boundaries of several European nations. At the conference, the Austrian diplomat Klemens von Metternich confirmed Habsburg control of land in central and eastern Europe. The independent archbishop's see of Salzburg and the Republic of Venice (now a part of Italy) also became Austrian territory. A German confederation (union of states), led by Austria, replaced the Holy Roman Empire.

THE AGE OF METTERNICH

After the Congress of Vienna, Metternich became the most powerful official in Austria. By limiting political activity and by restricting freedom of the press, he hoped to stop any opposition to the Habsburg dynasty.

At this time, new industries were drawing a large working class to Austrian cities. Many of the laborers lived in crowded and unhealthy housing, and factory wages were low. In the manufacturing centers of Vienna, Linz, and Graz, the workers, who allied themselves with Austria's peasants, began to demand changes in the Habsburg government.

Ferdinand I became the Austrian emperor in 1835. A weak ruler, he allowed his relatives to run Austria's various ministries. Rivalries among the members of the Habsburg family slowed the government's attempts to improve wages and working conditions. By the mid-1840s, an economic crisis and food shortages were causing widespread revolts among Austrian peasants and workers. University students joined the laborers in demanding a new government with a written constitution. Metternich, as the chief minister, faced strong popular and political opposition. In 1848 he resigned his post and fled to Britain.

A more liberal government replaced Metternich's administration and established a representative assembly called the Reichstag. This legislature freed the peas-

Independent Picture Service

Street riots in Vienna, prompted by widespread hunger and unemployment, brought about the downfall of the Austrian emperor Ferdinand I in 1848.

ants of their remaining obligations to landowners. But the Reichstag failed to agree
on other new laws. When street riots re-
sumed in Vienna, Ferdinand I fled the capital. In October 1848, forces loyal to the
Habsburgs invaded Vienna, putting a violent end to the street demonstrations. In
December Ferdinand's family and advisers
persuaded him to give up his throne in
favor of his nephew, Franz Joseph.

Franz Joseph

A strong-willed leader, Franz Joseph abol-
ished the Reichstag and restored the authority of the Habsburg ministers. In 1855
he returned Austrian schools to Roman
Catholic control. The emperor also re-
quested Russian troops to help put down
a rebellion in Hungary.

Although Franz Joseph had firm control
of domestic affairs, his foreign policy led
to many unsuccessful wars. The empire

Photo by Bettmann Archive

**Franz Joseph kept strict control over Austria's parliament
but agreed to the division of the Habsburg realm into the
dual monarchy of Austria-Hungary.**

Independent Picture Service

A funeral procession leaves Mayerling, a hunting lodge in the Vienna Woods, after a royal scandal occurred there
in 1889. In despair over a doomed romance, the crown prince Rudolf – Emperor Franz Joseph's son and heir –
committed suicide at the lodge. The tragedy rocked the Austrian government and was a severe blow to Franz Joseph.

29

Courtesy of Minneapolis Public Library and Information Center

Schönbrunn Palace, completed in 1730, was the summer residence of the Habsburgs. In 1805 and again in 1809, the French emperor Napoleon established his headquarters here while his armies occupied Vienna. The last Habsburg ruler, Charles I, announced his resignation at Schönbrunn in 1918.

lost territory after several Italian states fought for and won their independence in 1859. A defeat by Prussian armies in 1866 forced Austria to give up its leadership of the German Confederation. Prussia emerged as the leader of a new German empire, which became the strongest state in central Europe.

By 1867 these setbacks and new demonstrations in Austrian cities forced Franz Joseph to accept another representative assembly, the Reichsrat. This legislature decreed basic civil rights for all Austrian citizens and in 1907 extended the vote to all male Austrians. New laws permitted laborers to form trade unions, which had the right to call strikes to protest working conditions.

In 1867 Franz Joseph also reached an agreement with Hungarian leaders to establish a separate Hungarian constitution and monarchy. The Austrian Empire thus became Austria-Hungary, a union of two separate but equal kingdoms. In 1882 Austria-Hungary joined the Triple Alliance with Germany and Italy. The members of this new alliance sought to defend their borders against territorial expansion by Russia and France.

CONFLICTS WITHIN THE EMPIRE

After winning more civil rights in the late 1800s, Austrians founded new political parties. The Liberals represented Austria's growing middle class. The Christian Socialist party included peasants and members of the working class who supported the Roman Catholic Church. The Social Democratic party fought for changes in the economic system and for state ownership of private industries.

The Reichsrat faced the growing demands of the many separate ethnic groups that lived within Austria. Czechs, Slavs, Poles, and other groups wanted to form governments of their own. Legislation to grant more independence to these nationalities, however, failed to win the backing of the various parties or of the emperor. But Austria's ethnic minorities had the support of Russia and the new state of Serbia in southeastern Europe. This situation caused increasing mistrust and conflict among Austria, Russia, and Serbia in the early 1900s.

Relations between Austria and Serbia worsened after Austria took over one of Serbia's neighboring states in 1908. The Austrian action frustrated Serbia's goal of bringing this territory under Serbian control. The tension erupted into violence in 1914, when a Serbian assassinated Archduke Franz Ferdinand. Alliances made in the 1800s quickly brought nearly all of Europe into the conflict known as World War I. Within weeks, Austria and Germany were fighting against the combined forces of Britain, France, Serbia, Italy, and Russia—together called the Allies.

World War I and the Republic

By 1916 military defeats and food shortages were causing widespread discontent among Austrian civilians and soldiers. After the death of Emperor Franz Joseph in 1916, Charles I succeeded to the Habsburg throne. In the next year, Austrian workers protested worsening economic conditions. As the central government weakened, Poles, Czechs, Hungarians, and Slavs seized the chance to proclaim their independence from Habsburg control.

Austrian and German armies continued to lose ground, and in 1918 the two powers surrendered to the Allies. After this defeat, Charles I officially withdrew from the government, ending the 600-year reign of the Habsburg dynasty. A temporary assembly, led by the Social Democratic party, immediately declared the founding of the Republic of Austria. The Treaty of Saint-Germain, signed by Austria and the Allies in 1919, established the republic's present-day boundaries. The treaty also recognized Czechoslovakia, Hungary, and Yugoslavia as independent countries.

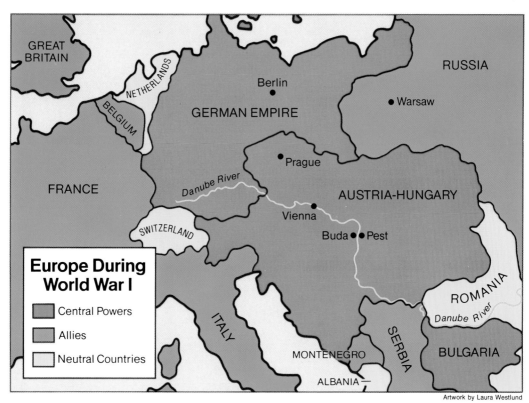

Artwork by Laura Westlund

By the summer of 1914, the Austrian Empire ruled ethnic minorities in central and southeastern Europe. Many of these peoples were demanding independence, yet the Habsburgs kept a firm hold on their possessions, which included Bosnia, Herzegovina, and land inhabited by the Czechs. Conflict between the Austrian government and Serbia, a nation that supported the region's independence movements, sparked the global conflict known as World War I.

In 1920 the Austrian assembly, made up of Social Democrats and Christian Socialists, passed a new constitution that created an elected legislature called the Nationalrat (National Council). The leader of the Nationalrat's majority party became the chancellor, or head of the government.

Unrest in Austria continued, however, as the republic's economy steadily declined. Conflict between the two main political parties often erupted in street battles fought by armed militias. Many Austrians felt that their country, now a fraction of the size of the old Habsburg Empire, could not survive as a separate state. Support for union (*Anschluss* in German) with Germany gained strength in the early 1930s. A worldwide economic depression and the collapse of an important bank in Vienna caused mass unemployment and further

Photo by Bettmann Archive

Unemployed laborers thronged the streets of Vienna in the 1920s. Poverty and joblessness in many European capitals caused popular discontent, encouraging new, authoritarian leaders and private armies, such as the Austrian Heimwehr.

Pedestrians cross a temporary walkway over the Danube canal in Vienna in 1945. Allied bombing destroyed many historic buildings, as well as factories and bridges, in the capital.

hardships. These problems strengthened the Anschluss movement.

In Germany, the popularity of Adolf Hitler and his National Socialist (or Nazi) party brought new pressure on the Austrian government to unite with Germany. A Nazi party formed in Austria, supported by a private army called the Heimwehr. Anti-Semitism (prejudice against Jewish people) was an important belief among members of both the German and Austrian Nazi parties.

The Heimwehr tried to overthrow the Austrian government in 1934. During the fighting, members of the Heimwehr killed the Christian Socialist chancellor, Engelbert Dollfuss. His successor, Kurt von Schuschnigg, allowed Nazi party members to head some of the state ministries.

These efforts did not satisfy Hitler, who in 1938 ordered German armies to invade Austria and put the Anschluss into effect by force. Austrian and German Nazi units arrested many political opponents and Jewish residents, sending them to concentration camps in Germany and Poland. Germany's invasion of Poland in 1939 brought Austria and much of the rest of Europe into World War II (1939–1945).

World War II and Modern Austria

Austria, Italy, and Germany—known as the Axis powers—fought World War II

33

against the allied forces of Britain, France, and the Soviet Union (formerly Russia). The United States entered the war on the side of the Allies in 1941. In 1943, after several early successes, the Axis nations began to lose territory. Allied planes bombed Austria, and the Soviet army invaded in 1945. By the end of the war in 1945, the fighting had damaged many Austrian cities and industries. British, U.S., French, and Soviet forces remained in the country, dividing it into four occupation zones.

After the war, a temporary administration headed by Karl Renner established the second Austrian republic. The government was run by a coalition (combination) of parties. It consisted of the Socialist (formerly Social Democratic) party, the People's (formerly Christian Socialist) party, and the Communist party. The Communists had close ties with the Soviet Union. Coalition governments continued to hold power

until the 1960s, but the Communist party lost much of its influence after the 1940s.

Disputes between the Soviet Union and the other allied nations divided postwar Europe into Western and Eastern blocs. The Eastern bloc came under the influence of the Soviet Union. The Western bloc remained allied with the other three victors of World War II—Britain, France, and the United States. Austria's location in central Europe—and its occupation by all four of the allied powers—placed it directly between the two opposing blocs.

Foreign aid and postwar economic planning helped Austria to rebuild its cities and industries. Trade unions, employers, and the government agreed on wages and prices, and these efforts aided the country's economic recovery. Yet for 10 years after the war, the occupying powers could not settle on the terms of a treaty that would again make Austria independent.

The Austrian coat of arms features the traditional Austrian eagle, an ancient symbol of the Habsburg Empire. On the eagle's head is a civic crown, representing the nation's prosperous middle class. The sickle and hammer held in the bird's talons represent the country's farmers and workers, respectively. Broken chains symbolize freedom gained after the end of World War II.

Artwork by Laura Westlund

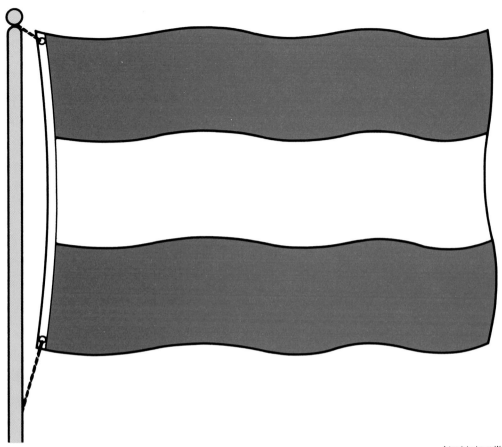

According to tradition, the colors of the Austrian flag originated in the clothing of the Austrian duke Leopold V of Babenberg. Leopold, a twelfth-century crusader, fought bravely and suffered so many wounds that his garments were stained red, except for a small white area. This flag has been the symbol of the Republic of Austria since the state's founding in 1918.

In the spring of 1955, the Soviet Union finally set forth economic and political conditions for leaving the country. Austria had to pay war damages to the Soviet government. Austria also agreed to follow a neutral policy, meaning the country would not take sides in any future military campaign. In May 1955, Austria signed the Treaty of State with the occupying nations, which then withdrew their forces.

In 1966 the People's party won a majority of seats in the Nationalrat. The 1970 elections brought the Socialists to power under Bruno Kreisky. The Socialists retained control of the government in the 1975 and 1979 elections.

Recent Events

The Kreisky government maintained a healthy Austrian economy despite a worldwide recession in the early 1970s. The international downturn resulted partly from rises in the cost of fuel, much of which Austria must buy from foreign countries. The need to import fuel also brought about a sharp debate within Austria over the use of nuclear power to generate electricity. A national vote in 1978 blocked the start-up of the country's only nuclear power plant.

Elections in 1983 ended the Socialist majority in the legislature. With the support of a third party, Fred Sinowatz then succeeded Kreisky as chancellor. A vote in 1986 renewed the coalition government between the Socialist and the People's parties. Franz Vranitzky, a moderate Socialist, became chancellor. He retained this post after the Socialists won a majority in the 1990 parliamentary elections.

Although Austria has maintained its military neutrality, the country has joined the United Nations (UN) and the European Free Trade Association (EFTA). Austria has also applied for membership in the European Community (EC), an economic partnership of European nations. As part of the EC, Austria would have a wider market in which to sell its goods. EC membership could also stimulate Austrian agriculture and manufacturing, helping the country to maintain a high standard of living for its people in the coming decades.

Government

After World War II, Austria reinstated the country's 1920 constitution, which had been suspended from 1938 to 1945 during the Anschluss with Germany. This constitution established Austria as a federal republic—an association of separate provinces under a central authority. The government consists of executive, legislative, and judicial branches.

Every six years, Austrians vote to elect the country's president, who heads the executive branch and commands the armed

Photo by Bettmann Archive

In 1974 Chancellor Bruno Kreisky *(left)* met with United Nations (UN) secretary-general Kurt Waldheim, who is also Austrian. While running for the Austrian presidency in 1986, Waldheim was accused of serving with a German security unit that committed atrocities during World War II. Waldheim denied the charges and won the election. The continuing controversy, however, has made Waldheim's role as president increasingly difficult.

forces. The president, however, does not have the power to stop legislation passed by the Nationalrat.

The Nationalrat and the Bundesrat (Federal Council) make up the Austrian parliament. The country's principal lawmaking assembly, the Nationalrat has 183 members who are elected to four-year terms. After these national elections, the president appoints a member of the legislature's majority party as the country's chancellor. The chancellor leads the government and the cabinet, which is made up of the heads of governmental ministries.

The legislatures of the country's nine provinces elect the Bundesrat's 54 members. These representatives serve terms lasting from four to six years. The Bundesrat can propose laws and must approve the country's international treaties and agreements.

Austria's supreme court is the country's highest court. Several provincial and lower courts also hear important cases. Special courts judge cases involving administrative, constitutional, labor, and juvenile disputes.

Voters in each of Austria's nine provinces elect a Landtag, or provincial legislature. Members of the Landtag appoint the governor of the province as well as

A successful banker before gaining his post in 1986, Chancellor Franz Vranitzky has forged close ties with the nation's business community.

representatives to the Bundesrat. The Landtags also create laws for their own provinces, although a federal ministry must approve them. The provincial legislatures set minimum voting ages for all Austrian elections.

Austrian cities and villages make up more than 2,000 communes, which elect governing councils. These councils debate local issues and appoint the burgomaster, or mayor of the commune.

The Austrian parliament, built in Vienna between 1873 and 1883, houses both the Nationalrat and the Bundesrat. Behind the parliament rises the spire of the capital's city hall.

Photo by Drs. A. A. M. van der Heyden, Naarden, the Netherlands

3) The People

Since 1980 Austria's population has remained stable at about 7.7 million. If the country maintains its very low population growth rate of .1 percent, the number of inhabitants will not double for 770 years. Austria's birthrate—12 births for every 1,000 people—is one of the world's lowest.

Deaths during World War II, the shattered postwar economy, and emigration contributed to the country's low birthrate in the 1940s and 1950s. As a result, much

of Austria's population is either under 24 or over 65 years of age. This high percentage of very young and very old people places a heavy burden on Austria's health and educational systems.

Ethnic Groups

Although most Austrians are of German stock, their ethnic heritage reflects the invasions and migrations that took place

Once a royal game preserve, the Prater is now a popular amusement park lying near the Danube River in Vienna. A British architect designed the Prater's famous Ferris wheel—one of the world's first such structures—in 1897.

during the country's early history. Before the Habsburgs came to power in the 1200s, Celts, Romans, Germans, Magyars, and Slavs built settlements along Austria's rivers and in the mountain valleys. In later centuries, Croats, Slovenes, and Hungarians moved into Burgenland, Carinthia, and Styria. Intermarriage between ethnic groups occurred in the northern and eastern provinces, where better roads and the

Sled races are a popular pastime in many Austrian villages and towns. Horse-drawn sleds were once a useful means of travel during the snowy Alpine winters.

Danube River allowed easy travel and settlement. The mountainous provinces of Tyrol, Vorarlberg, and Salzburg remained mostly German.

A majority of Austrians now live in the Danube Valley and in the eastern half of the country. About 56 percent inhabit urban areas. After World War II, immigrants and political refugees came from Yugoslavia, Czechoslovakia, and Hungary, Austria's eastern European neighbors. During the 1980s, nearly 200,000 foreign workers, mostly from the poorer countries of Turkey and Yugoslavia, sought work as unskilled laborers in Austrian cities.

Health and Education

The Austrian government spends nearly one-third of its budget on social welfare, health care, and new housing. All Austrian workers participate in an insurance program that guarantees financial aid in case of accident, sickness, or disability. The program also includes old-age pensions, which now benefit nearly two million people. Employers, employees, and the government contribute to national health insurance, which covers all workers and their families.

Austria has more than 22,000 physicians —an average of 1 for every 428 people. This figure represents one of the world's

Photo by Bernice K. Condit

On a Sunday afternoon, villagers of Kals in Carinthia dress in traditional costumes for a local festival.

highest doctor-to-patient ratios. The country also ranks high in the number of hospital beds, an important measure of health standards. Infant mortality—the number of babies who die during the first year of life—is 8 per 1,000, an average figure among western European countries. The extensive health services available to Austrians have helped them to achieve a high average life expectancy of 75 years.

Since 1774 Austria has provided its citizens with free public education. The country's literacy rate—the percentage of adults who can read and write—has reached 99 percent. All children between the ages of 6 and 15 must attend school. The first four school years take place in a *Volksschule,* or primary school. After the Volksschule, some students continue their education in a secondary school for eight years. When these students are about 18, they must pass a difficult examination before they can enter a university. Other students leaving the Volksschule enter a four-year *Hauptschule,* then receive four more years of training at a technical or vocational institute. Some of these schools also prepare students for university education.

Austria's largest and oldest institution of higher learning is the University of Vienna, which enrolls more than 30,000 students. Founded in 1365, it was one of the first universities established in the German-speaking world. Specialized colleges prepare students for professions in law, medicine, and business. Six fine-arts colleges also offer courses. Many workers over the age of 24 continue their job training at adult education centers.

Language and Literature

Nearly all Austrians use German as their first language. The Austrian dialect, which German-speakers from other nations can easily understand, has many foreign words and phrases in its vocabulary. Some inhabitants of Burgenland use Hungarian. Many of the 20,000 Slovenes living in Carinthia

Independent Picture Service

Heinrich von Ferstel designed the central building of the University of Vienna in 1873. The Austrian physician Sigmund Freud, the university's most famous professor, taught here from 1902 until 1938.

Courtesy of Library of Congress

Sigmund Freud explained his theories about the subconscious mind in a series of books describing the dreams, fears, and personal lives of his patients.

41

Photo by Bettmann Archive

Hugo von Hofmannsthal (1874–1929) wrote several plays in verse as well as poetry. Many of his works, including *Elektra, Der Rosenkavalier,* and *Ariadne auf Naxos,* were set to music by the German composer Richard Strauss.

send their children to separate schools where classes are taught in Slovenian, an eastern European tongue.

Austria's earliest literature took the form of epic stories, such as the *Niebelungenlied,* that were sung in German by court poets called minnesingers. These performers entertained royalty with tales of love and the deeds of heroes, giants, and monsters. The poetry of Walther von der Vogelweide, a celebrated thirteenth-century minnesinger, became famous throughout the German-speaking world. The nobleman Hugo von Montfort (1377–1445) preferred to write about the people and problems of his time.

After the Thirty Years' War, Austrian writers borrowed many of the literary forms popular in the Catholic nations of Italy and Spain. In the 1700s, magic plays with symbolic figures and supernatural events were popular among both royalty and the common people. A well-known play, *The Magic Flute* by Emanuel Schikaneder, became one of the first German-language operas when Wolfgang Amadeus Mozart set it to music in 1791.

Franz Grillparzer (1791–1872) wrote plays as well as long poems based on Austria's history. Among his most famous works is *King Ottokar's Rise and Fall,* a play about the life of Ottokar II, who was defeated in battle by Rudolf of Habsburg. Grillparzer's skill at recreating history in the form of poetry made him one of Austria's most popular writers.

Adalbert Stifter, who lived at the same time as Grillparzer, celebrated Austrian middle-class life in his novels. The stories and plays of Arthur Schnitzler, who began his career as a doctor, explore human emotions and psychology. Hugo von Hofmannsthal, a playwright and poet of the early 1900s, used a variety of themes in his work. Many of his stories take the form of traditional legends, while others borrow from Greek mythology and drama. Hofmannsthal wrote several librettos (scripts) for the operas of the German composer Richard Strauss.

The Austrian physician Sigmund Freud, who lived in Vienna until the 1930s, had a strong impact on Austrian writers and artists of the twentieth century. Freud's ideas about the subconscious mind influenced Stefan Zweig, whose biographies of historical figures rely on psychological analysis. Robert Musil's book *The Man Without Qualities* examines Austrian society during the 1930s.

In his long novels, Heimito von Doderer described Viennese life in the years after World War II. Peter Handke, a well-known contemporary author, tries new writing techniques in his experimental novels and in his scripts for theater, movies, and television.

Music

Austria's earliest known musical works are religious hymns and chants that were performed in churches and monasteries during the Babenberg dynasty. The lyric poetry of the twelfth-century minnesingers, who accompanied themselves with a variety of instruments, was also popular among the Babenberg rulers.

Between the fourteenth and sixteenth centuries, German musicians came to Austria to lead choirs and instrumental groups. In the 1600s, Italian music became fashionable. Austrian composers were soon combining Italian styles with Austrian folk tunes to create *Singspiele*—light-hearted plays that included popular songs.

The support of royalty and rich nobles allowed music to flourish in Vienna and in other Austrian cities in the eighteenth century. Joseph Haydn, who worked for the wealthy prince Miklós József Esterházy, wrote symphonies and sonatas

Photo by Foto Fayer

One of the world's leading orchestras, the Vienna Philharmonic performs in the restored National Opera House in central Vienna. Many of the orchestra's concerts are sold out well in advance of the concert date.

43

Wolfgang Amadeus Mozart performed for royalty and aristocrats but died in poverty while struggling to earn a living in Vienna.

—musical forms still used by modern composers. Haydn published many of his works during his lifetime and became one of Europe's most popular composers.

Mozart, a performer who dazzled court audiences while still a boy, created more than 600 compositions, including brilliant operas, symphonies, and instrumental sonatas. Many of his works received critical acclaim, but musicians and singers found Mozart's music difficult to perform. After struggling to support himself, Mozart died in poverty at the age of 35.

Although born in Germany, Ludwig van Beethoven (1770–1827) spent most of his adult life in Vienna. Beethoven's compositions and piano concerts brought him fame among the Viennese. At the height of his career, however, Beethoven began to lose his hearing and became unable to perform in public. Despite his deafness, he continued to write expressive and powerful music that influenced later composers throughout Europe.

Franz Schubert (1797–1828) wrote hundreds of works for piano, orchestra, and chamber ensembles (small groups of instruments). His most popular pieces were lieder (songs) arranged for voice and piano.

Ludwig van Beethoven, 14 years younger than Mozart, commanded respect from patrons, audiences, and music publishers. By the time of his death in 1827, Beethoven's compositions were famous throughout Europe.

This monument to Johann Strauss, Jr., stands in a Viennese park. Strauss wrote music in many different forms but is most famous for his graceful waltzes.

Independent Picture Service

Architects working in the baroque style designed the Grand Gallery in Schönbrunn, the summer palace of the Habsburgs. Ornate chandeliers, ceiling paintings, and intricately carved woodwork are all hallmarks of baroque decoration.

Both Gustav Mahler and Anton Bruckner created long, dramatic symphonies in the late nineteenth century. Johann Strauss and his son Johann Strauss, Jr., composed lighter music for the Viennese waltz, a popular dance. Franz von Suppé and Franz Lehár wrote operettas that are still popular in Vienna.

Austria's twentieth-century composers invented and refined new composing techniques. Arnold Schönberg, Alban Berg, and Anton von Webern created operas and orchestral pieces without using traditional musical harmonies. Other composers continued to use the forms pioneered by Haydn. Erich Wolfgang Korngold wrote popular songs, musicals, and film scores. Both light opera and more serious concert music still thrive in Austria.

Visual Arts

In the early centuries of Habsburg rule, Austrian architects used building techniques imported from other parts of Europe. The designers of St. Stephen's Cathedral in Vienna, for example, employed the gothic style from France. By the late 1600s, the Habsburgs were inviting Italian architects to Austria to design churches and palaces. The baroque style used by the Italians favored large-scale structures and extravagant decoration. Other builders added wood, marble, and gold ornaments to create a distinctive style known as Austrian baroque.

Johann Fischer von Erlach, who designed the Karlskirche and many other baroque buildings in Vienna, used both French and Italian forms in his work. The rococo style

45

of the late 1700s marked Austrian churches of the time with elaborate painting and sculpture. Many Austrian architects of the early 1800s rejected the rococo style and used the simpler forms of ancient Greek and Roman buildings in their designs.

Adolph Loos, who worked in the late nineteenth and early twentieth centuries, used simple, clear lines and flat surfaces in the design of offices and apartment buildings. Otto Wagner, a contemporary of Loos, designed several large public buildings in Vienna. Wagner's modern style caused controversy among those who preferred traditional architecture.

Most Austrian painters of the seventeenth and eighteenth centuries imitated German baroque artists. The Austrians depicted religious and mythological scenes on church altars and on palace walls and ceilings. In the early 1800s, Austrian artists turned away from these traditional subjects, focusing instead on nature and on scenes of family life.

At the turn of the twentieth century, several Austrian painters contributed to

Many baroque churches contain ceilings, walls, altars, and statues decorated with thin layers of gold. This gilded statue of Saint George was made for a church in Styria.

Courtesy of Austrian National Tourist Office

Villagers and livestock decorated with flowers and bells parade through the streets of a Tyrolean village.

new artistic movements. Gustav Klimt conveyed the emotions of his subjects through unusual symbols, colors, and designs. The expressive and disturbing paintings of Egon Schiele and Oskar Kokoschka reflected a time of social tension and uncertainty.

Austrian craftspeople have also excelled in woodcarving, ironworking, tapestry weaving, and porcelain production. The export of these traditional handicrafts remains an important part of the Austrian economy.

Religion and Festivals

About 90 percent of Austrians belong to the Roman Catholic Church, which is financially supported by the state. Nevertheless, the country's laws guarantee freedom of religion. Six percent of Austrians are members of various Protestant communities. Eastern Christian sects, such as the Greek Orthodox and Russian Orthodox

Courtesy of Austrian National Tourist Office

Austrians adorn small chapels and traditional trees with lights and trimmings during the Christmas season.

47

The phantom dance is a rite of Fasching, an Austrian spring festival. Dancers wear costumes and unusual hats while parading through villages to celebrate the passing of winter.

Shortly before Christmas, according to tradition, good Austrian children receive gifts from Saint Nicholas. Bad children, however, are teased by monsters, such as this *krampusse* strolling through a Styrian town.

churches, still draw many worshipers who immigrated to Austria from eastern Europe. Most Jewish people left the country or died during the 1930s and 1940s, when the Nazis controlled Austria. Jews now number about 12,000, with the majority living in Vienna.

Austrians observe religious and national holidays with parades and feasting. During the spring festival of Fasching, people wearing costumes to celebrate winter's passing march through mountain villages. In late June on Midsummer Day, bonfires light up cities and towns. Fall harvest festivals in rural villages mark the end of the growing season. On October 26, Austrians celebrate the anniversary of the day the allied powers ended their postwar occupation in 1955.

Austria's Christmas season begins on December 5, when Saint Nicholas appears in the streets, offering cakes and candies to children. The season ends on Epiphany, a Christian holiday on January 6. On the eve of Epiphany, children dressed as biblical figures pass from house to house, singing a folk song and blessing homes for the new year.

These antique barrels hold Austrian white wine. Each fall, just after the harvest, new wine arrives in special taverns called *Heuriger*. The tavern owners serve the refreshing, sweet heuriger wines straight from the barrel.

Food

Austria's history as a large, multi-ethnic empire has brought great variety to the nation's cuisine. Each Austrian province boasts a local specialty. Pastries from Vienna, as well as Viennese coffee, are famous throughout Europe. Wiener schnitzel, a thin slice of breaded veal, is a Viennese recipe that has become the country's most popular meat dish.

Hot or cold noodles are often accompanied by a variety of meats and vegetables in a popular Carinthian specialty. Tyroleans make tasty cheeses, and Austrian cooks use Tyrolean smoked bacon in

soups, salads, and dumplings. Vineyards in the province of Lower Austria, and in the Danube River Valley, produce grapes for many of the country's sweet white wines.

Breakfast in Austria usually consists of coffee or milk, accompanied by bread with butter and marmalade. In the middle of the morning, Austrians sometimes snack on small sausages served with mustard on a hard roll.

The noon meal is traditionally the heaviest of the day. Soup is followed by a main course of meat or fish. Beef, pork, chicken, sausage, and veal are popular entrees. Austrians serve fresh vegetables and noodles, potatoes, or dumplings with the main course, which is often followed by a salad. In the midafternoon comes a short break for coffee and a rich dessert, such as Linzer torte. The *Kaffeehaus* (coffee shop) is a popular place for afternoon socializing in Austrian cities.

The evening meal is traditionally lighter than the noon meal. This *Abendessen* (supper) often includes cold meats, cheese, and smoked fish prepared on open-faced sandwiches. During the cold winter months, soups and stews are sometimes served in the evening.

Sports and Recreation

Austria's mountains, forests, and lakes provide many opportunities for outdoor sports. People living in mountainous regions often rely on skiing for everyday transportation. Resorts in Kitzbühel and

Paprika chicken *(left)*, potato noodles *(top)*, and a mixed green salad are popular items for a festive dinner. This meal begins with egg custard soup *(bottom)*.

River rafting is a popular and exciting sport on the rushing waterways of the Austrian Alps.

the Inn Valley in Tyrol draw skiers from around the world. The country has also produced several Olympic skiing champions. Anton (Toni) Sailer, a skier from Kitzbühel, swept the Winter Olympics' three downhill races in 1956. Franz Klammer won a gold medal in downhill racing in 1976.

Many Austrian skiers begin their training at a young age. These children are following their instructor along a special *Kinderskikurs,* or children's ski run, at an Alpine resort.

The Salzkammergut, near Austria's border with Germany, is a water-sports paradise. The clear, calm waters of the Mondsee, Attersee, Wolfgangsee and other lakes in the region are ideal for waterskiing.

Cross-country ski trails follow the mountain valleys in western and southern Austria, and toboggan runs have been built near many Alpine resorts. Ice-skating is popular on the frozen lakes and rivers. Curling, a game played by sliding a heavy stone along a flat surface of ice, is a popular cold-weather team sport.

In the summer, the lakes of Austria attract many boaters, swimmers, waterskiers, and fishing enthusiasts. Hiking and camping are favorite activities in the mountains. Football (soccer) is the nation's most popular team sport. Austria's national football team has competed in both European and World Cup championships.

A lone hiker explores the tricky crevasses of the Pasterze Glacier. Behind the glacier rises the imposing peak of Grossglockner (12,460 ft.), Austria's highest point. Slowed by the mountain's steep slopes and high winds, climbers did not reach the summit of Grossglockner until July 1800.

This factory worker prepares engine parts in an auto plant. Car manufacturers from the United States have established new facilities in partnership with the Austrian government and with other private businesses.

Courtesy of General Motors Austria Gesellschaft

4) The Economy

Austria once had a largely agricultural economy. In the early 1800s, however, factories began to draw workers from the countryside to the cities. Steel and textiles became important exports, and railroads and river barges improved transportation of goods to market. In the late 1930s, Austrian industry became an important source of weaponry for Germany.

But bombing during World War II damaged many Austrian factories. After the war, Soviet authorities dismantled some plants and shipped heavy equipment to the Soviet Union. From 1945 until the end of the allied occupation in 1955, most new factories were built in western Austria. Older plants continued to operate in Soviet-occupied eastern Austria.

In the late 1940s, to aid the country's economic recovery, the Austrian government took control of the transportation network and major industries. Austrian

Vineyards along the Danube supply white-wine grapes to Austrian vintners (winemakers). The Danube River Valley and the Vienna Basin region have been centers of Austrian winemaking for more than 1,000 years.

workers organized the Austrian Trade Union Federation, which met with government ministers to set wages, prices, and labor policies. The continuing cooperation between the Austrian government and Austrian workers has resulted in stable prices and low unemployment.

In the late 1980s, certain large industries, such as oil refining and iron-ore mining, remained under government super-vision. Other firms, such as the national airline, were privatized, meaning that the government permitted private investors to buy shares of the companies. This arrangement allowed managers of the privatized firms to set prices and wages with less governmental interference. The privatized companies face increased competition from foreign companies, however, and must survive without government support.

The murals decorating this store in Vienna were painted in the art nouveau style, which was popular among Austrian artists during the early twentieth century.

Steelmaking has long been an important Austrian industry. While older plants still operate in Lower Austria and near Vienna, newer operations, such as this factory in the village of Mürzzuschlag in Styria, have been established in other parts of the country.

Manufacturing

Manufacturing is Austria's leading economic activity, employing nearly a third of the country's labor force. Vienna, Graz, and Linz have become centers of steelmaking and chemical production. Workers in smaller factories throughout Austria weave textiles, process minerals, and make handicrafts.

Abundant supplies of iron ore are important to the production of steel and iron, traditional industries in the Mur and Mürz river valleys of Styria. Large plants in Linz and Donawitz fashion steel parts for vehicles and weaponry. After suffering financial losses in the early 1980s, the steel industry was partially privatized in 1985.

At the same time, many Austrians were protesting the high levels of air pollution in their cities. In the late 1980s, the steel companies invested in new equipment to reduce the polluting smoke emitted by

Factory engineers adjust a machine that makes fine-quality paper.

their plants. Although their operations have become cleaner and more profitable, Austrian steelmakers now face competition from eastern Europe, where new governments are modernizing heavy industry.

Large factories in Vienna and in the surrounding region make heavy machinery, automobiles, buses, railway cars, and trucks. A new plant in Styria assembles vehicles designed in the United States. Foreign companies have established other factories in Austria to make car engines.

The chemical industry, which is centered in Linz, produces fertilizers, plastics, rubber goods, and industrial chemicals. Modernized plants and new equipment have improved production methods, and Austrian chemical companies have set up research centers to develop new fertilizers and drugs.

For centuries, textiles have been an important industry in Vorarlberg. Textile exports rose rapidly during the 1800s, when new machines improved the spinning and weaving processes. Although much of this equipment is now outdated, Austria still exports Vorarlberg's woven fabrics and finished clothing.

Beverages and processed foods are another important export industry in Austria, although this business is subject to intense competition and high tariffs (import taxes). Many of the country's wines, such as Riesling and Gumpoldskirchner, are popular abroad.

Independent Picture Service

Textile machinery operates in an Austrian clothing mill. Cloth production, which was once done entirely by hand on manual looms, now benefits from the speed and accuracy of automated spinning and weaving.

Agriculture and Forestry

Agriculture and forestry, which have declined in importance in the Austrian economy, now employ about 6 percent of the country's workers. Although only 20 percent of Austria's land is suitable for crops, modern methods and equipment allow farmers to supply 90 percent of the nation's food. Farms average about 25 acres in size, and nearly all of them are privately owned.

The lower elevations of northern Austria support both crops and livestock. Potatoes, barley, wheat, corn, and oats are the principal food crops. Fruit orchards, wine grapes, and tobacco also thrive in northern and eastern Austria.

Pastures in the high mountain valleys, where the growing season is too short for crops, supply enough forage for herds of dairy and beef cattle. Austrian farmers also raise pigs, sheep, chickens, and horses, and

A woodcutter poses with a pile of rough-cut logs. The reforestation of Austrian land since World War II has provided new resources for the paper and construction industries. In addition, many Alpine farmers who cannot profitably grow crops plant trees for harvest instead.

Photo © David Falconer

the nation is self-sufficient in meat and dairy products. Farms in remote and mountainous regions, however, are suffering from a shortage of labor as rural people move to the cities. To survive, some farmers must add to their income by doing nonagricultural work.

Heavy damage and overcutting of Austrian forests occurred during and after World War II. An extensive reforestation effort has been under way since the 1950s. Many farmers have planted their unproductive Alpine pastures with trees that have commercial value. Forests now cover about one-third of Austria's land. Spruce and fir, which make up most of the replanted forests, are used in the production of paper and packaging. Austria also produces lumber for the construction industry.

Photo by Drs. A. A. M. van der Heyden, Naarden, the Netherlands

The taverns that sell heuriger wine announce the arrival of the new vintage by hanging a vine from their establishments. Many tavern owners cultivate their own wine grapes on adjoining land.

Energy and Mining

Two-thirds of the electricity used in Austria comes from hydroelectric stations powered by the Danube and other fast-flowing rivers. During the summer, these stations produce a surplus of electricity that Austria exports. In the winter months, when river flow decreases, the country must import electricity.

Photo © Klaus Bayr/Visuals Unlimited

Lipizzaner stallions graze near Piber in Styria. These horses are bred for the famous Spanish Riding Academy in Vienna. Other breeds raised by Austrian farmers become workhorses or racehorses.

Austria's reserves of coal, oil, and natural gas are steadily declining. The country imports nearly 90 percent of its coal and oil, and about 75 percent of its natural gas. Engineers designed a nuclear power station at Zwentendorf, near Vienna, to supply more than 10 percent of the country's electricity needs. A vote by Austrian citizens in 1978, however, prevented the plant from starting its operation.

Iron ore is Austria's most important mineral resource. Many of the country's iron-ore mines, and the steel factories that they supply, are located in Styria. Lignite (low-grade coal), also from Styria, is burned to generate electricity at power plants. Magnesite, a fire-resistant ore used in many building materials, is an important export. Mining companies also extract and refine copper, lead, antimony, zinc, graphite, and salt.

An iron-ore miner drills through solid rock on the Erzberg, or "iron mountain," in Styria. Most of Austria's ore supplies steel factories in Linz or Donawitz.

The Erzberg, one of Europe's largest deposits of iron ore, has been an important resource since before the Roman occupation in the first century B.C. Surface mining has eroded the mountain's summit more than 600 feet since the late nineteenth century.

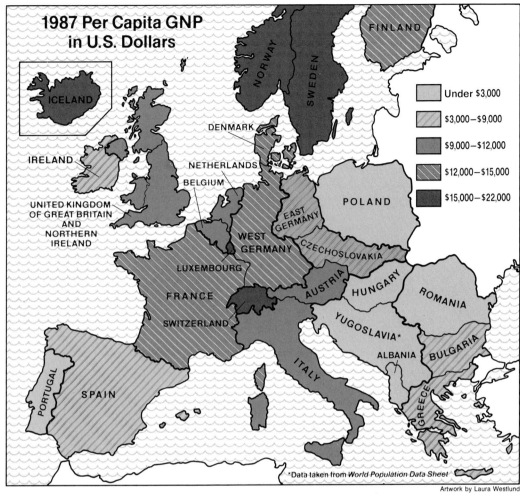

1987 Per Capita GNP in U.S. Dollars

	Under $3,000
	$3,000–$9,000
	$9,000–$12,000
	$12,000–$15,000
	$15,000–$22,000

ICELAND

NORWAY

SWEDEN

FINLAND

DENMARK

IRELAND

NETHERLANDS

BELGIUM

UNITED KINGDOM
OF GREAT BRITAIN
AND
NORTHERN
IRELAND

EAST
GERMANY

POLAND

WEST
GERMANY

CZECHOSLOVAKIA

LUXEMBOURG

AUSTRIA

HUNGARY

ROMANIA

FRANCE

SWITZERLAND

YUGOSLAVIA*

ALBANIA

BULGARIA

PORTUGAL

SPAIN

ITALY

GREECE

*Data taken from *World Population Data Sheet*

Artwork by Laura Westlund

This chart compares the average productivity per person—calculated by gross national product (GNP) per capita—for 26 European countries. The GNP is the value of all goods and services produced by a country in a year. To arrive at the GNP per capita, each nation's total GNP is divided by its population. The resulting dollar amounts indicate one measure of the standard of living in each country. Although it has benefited from a strong economy since the 1950s, Austria's per-capita GNP of $11,970 remains near the average figure for European countries. (Data taken from *Europa World Yearbook, 1989.*)

Foreign Trade

Austrian exports include lumber and paper products, chemicals, clothing, magnesite, steel, processed foods, wine, and machinery. Nearly half of all the country's exports go to Germany, and about 10 percent are purchased by Italy. Austria imports metal, food, petroleum, and high-grade coal. Germany, Italy, Japan, Switzerland, and France are the largest suppliers of imported goods.

As a member of the European Free Trade Association, Austria participates in a common market with Switzerland, Sweden, Finland, Norway, and Iceland. Nevertheless, Austria conducts most of its trade with the European Community (EC), a group of western European countries that follow common economic policies. In July 1989, Austria applied for EC membership. The country hopes to participate in the open market among EC nations planned for 1992.

Lipizzaner horses have become one of the capital's most popular tourist attractions. The graceful jumps and intricate parades are performed under the direction of the animals' uniformed trainers.

The Schloss Esterházy near Eisenstadt in Burgenland was the castle of a wealthy family that employed Joseph Haydn as a private court composer.

Tourism and Transportation

Austria's tourism brings in an average of $10 billion per year. Many regions, such as the western province of Tyrol, depend on tourism for much of their income and employment. About 18 million visitors, more than half of them from Germany, arrived annually in the early 1990s.

Among the country's most popular attractions are mountain resorts that offer winter and summer recreation in the western provinces. The lakes of Carinthia and of the Salzkammergut region also draw many visitors. The Austrian spas of Baden and Bad Ischl provide accommodation and the use of healthy mineral baths. Vienna has concerts, museums, restaurants, and historic palaces. An additional attraction in the capital are the intricate performances of the Lipizzaner horses, which are trained by members of the Spanish Riding Academy.

The town of Melk lies on the banks of the Danube River between Linz and Vienna. A fortified stronghold under the Babenberg rulers, Melk became the site of an imposing baroque monastery in the early eighteenth century. The domes and towers of the monastery rise from a steep bluff above the town's main square.

The tourism industry benefits from an extensive network of roads that connects major cities as well as remote mountain villages. A landlocked country, Austria also depends on its 7,000 miles of railway lines to move many of its exports. A canal linking the Danube with the Main and Rhine rivers in Germany will open in 1992. This canal will provide Austria with a new transportation route to Germany and to northwestern Europe. Six commercial airports, including Vienna's Schwechat, serve the national carrier—Austrian Airlines— as well as other international airlines.

The Future

Austria has made a strong recovery from the loss of its empire and from the damage done by two world wars. The country's coalition governments, which have held power in most years since the end of World War II, have rebuilt the economy and cooperated with labor leaders. Austrians now benefit from low unemployment, a stable administration, and a high standard of living. The new governments that are emerging in eastern Europe—especially those in Hungary and Czechoslovakia— could provide Austria with increasing trade opportunities. Membership in the EC would also create a larger market for Austrian products.

Austrians take pride in the spirit of cooperation that helped the country survive difficult times and attain prosperity. But to meet stronger European competition and to maintain its healthy economy, Austria must continue investing in and updating its industries.

Index